THE POLITICS OF TASTE

Karisma

Copyright © 2024 Karisma

All rights reserved.

ISBN code: 9798327303157

BUSINESS INQUIRIES
KARISMA.PRESS@GMAIL.COM

MEHR LICHT!

So Goethe passed away.

May this little essay enlighten one of your days and dispel the darkness of matter and perception.

THE CHAPTERS

	Thanks	V
1	OBJECTIVITY IN TASTE	6
2	STAR SYSTEM	11
3	THE EXTERMINATING ANGEL	27
4	ΚΑΛΌΣ ΚΑΊ ἈΓΑΘΌΣ	36
5	ANTI-INTELLIGENCE	39
6	DIVINE SPARK	45
7	NEBULOUS VIBRATIONS	49

DUE THANKS

First and foremost to the editorial team of Border Nights, who broadcast an excerpt of this Essay, narrated by me, on their main dissemination channels.

Secondly, to all of you. I'm grateful for your time and interest.

CHAPTER I

"OBJECTIVITY IN TASTE"

As Montesquieu asserted, there exist two categories of taste: the natural and the acquired.

Reasonably, I dare say, he argued that natural taste was that instinct which, by its very definition, unconsciously directs towards certain interests (reading, cinema, education, information), thereby giving rise to acquired taste.

However, what makes Montesquieu's theory particularly intriguing is the fact that the opposite appears to be even more truthful.

Acquired taste seeks to shape what is naturally deemed pleasing or akin to us, using one's interests as a tool and measure of evaluation to mold what, by nature, would be found interesting.

In support of this thesis, a personal experience comes to my aid, which I wish to share without indulging in sterile elitism: the reading of Dostoevsky's 'White Nights' or the science fiction works of Philip K. Dick, as well as the writings of Nabokov, E.M. Cioran, or Pasternak.

In these, and many other instances, I found myself compelled to admit that everything I had previously read needed to be reevaluated and reexamined under a more critical light (in the case of Dick, much of the science fiction transmitted and narrated in contemporary times had been anticipated by him in his visionary works. It is therefore difficult not to doze off in front of the latest Interstellar).

My taste underwent a considerable refinement.

I recall that it was necessary for the development of intellectual honesty in the field of criticism or the recognition of objectivity to establish points of comparison.

This appears obvious, almost taken for granted. Even a child accustomed to the modest churches of their own village would be amazed by the grandeur of St. Peter's or the Taj Mahal.

Therefore, once the premises of this truth are established, I can assert with certainty that there exists the possibility of refining one's taste and, consequently, recognizing something that intrinsically enjoys higher value.

Clearly, I do not mean to speak of taste in culinary terms—if one prefers a kiwi to a banana, that is a personal and indisputable preference.

I refer instead to the need to objectively judge a work of ingenuity according to certain criteria, for it is precisely objective criteria that we are discussing.

We must always remember that art is a human invention language, just like any other language, and therefore lives by its own rules.

A language that may not necessarily be understandable by everyone, like all other languages. For example, I do not know the French language. This does not make the French language any less objective or functional for communication.

However, attempting to pass off every language as an art is an act of great effrontery and audacity, despite the numerous attempts made to convince otherwise. "The art of military commands" has indeed entered the common imagination, hence the idea of 'The Art Of War' (Sun Tzu, 5th-4th century BC), hence the art of destruction.

Contrary to the avant-garde beliefs of the Italian futurists of the 20th century, for me, all this is as far away as it gets from what I define as art.

Death, annihilation, and the destruction of bodies and souls generate nothing.

And nothing cannot be considered art.

However, we must recognize that someone was certainly inspired by the atrocities of war. As in the case of Picasso with his 'Guernica' or Max Ernst with 'The Angel of Hearth and Home' (both 1937).

Anyway, despite the affection and admiration I might feel for the works in question, I would have preferred a world without them and without the annihilation of innocent people.

This degree of malignancy is not necessary to create.

In the same years, Giorgio Morandi painted incessantly still lifes, as if he were a stranger to the surrounding world, despite having lived through two world wars.

CHAPTER II

"STAR SYSTEM"

Established, therefore, it is necessary to recognize the existence of rules and objectivity in order to discuss or judge a work of art, my criticism becomes harsher towards those who deny the existence of the aforementioned.

In particular, I observe in this era a constant desire and need to mask one's cultural shortcomings behind Schopenhauer's so-called 'Veil of Maya', the veil of illusion.

The use of the fallacious, cowardly, and cowardly card of "subjectivity" by those who do not have the will or interest to deepen what they unconsciously sink into is becoming increasingly frequent.

Even to judge the kiwi mentioned earlier, it is necessary to preserve the integrity of one's taste, which could be compromised, for example, by a too high fever. For the same reason, I could not rely on a blind person to examine a painting.

The total absence of an artistic culture would not be a problem if it were not for the fact that a general cultural decay influences the quality of life of the individual, and consequently, therefore, the entire collective consciousness.

It is known, "thanks" also to the examples of past dictators, how powerful cinematographic means are in shaping the masses. (I recall that many of them were fans of Gustave Le Bon's literary work, 'The Crowd: A Study of the Popular Mind').

Even Hitler considered cinema the most effective means of propaganda, and it cannot be said that he was wrong or failed in his persuasion enterprise.

It is evident that a reduction in the quality of productions destined for the public inevitably leads to an ethical and moral decline, just as a diet of only sweets leads to the deterioration of teeth, and beyond.

Before proceeding with my personal harangue, it is essential to establish further solid presuppositions.

The first, crucial, is that the ruling class is ignorant.

For some reason unknown to me, it is presumed that those who govern not only act for our good but also have a knowledge superior to the average.

Perhaps it is true, but it is another form of knowledge, one that puts you on the easy path to "the armchair", while the path to truth and culture (to me) turns out to be the exact opposite.

The ruling class, if it ever wanted to effectively spread culture among the people, would not even know where to start.

And I emphasize "if ever wanted to".

There is no interest, capacity, or, above all, willingness on the part of the government (whatever it may be, given that by definition there is no magnanimous government) to educate and alphabetize people to true beauty.

Those in the "button room" (which is not, in any case, the government visible to us) are well aware of how dangerous a pure idea, an idea of freedom, an idea that spurs on research can be.

There is nothing new in this. No differently from how Machiavelli described government in 'The Prince' 500 years ago, I therefore consider every form of power a Machiavellian project (as amply demonstrated by the 'Milgram Experiment' of 1961 or the Stanford prison experiment conducted by Philip Zimbardo in 1971).

The second fundamental assumption is that people are unaware of how much of what they consider artistically relevant (especially TV series and music) is constructed, embellished, polished, and promoted to collectively lower their level of consciousness.

It's the product of the inverted pyramid of power, and it's tailor-made. Tailored to the masses. It's a bespoke suit designed not to protect them but to contain them - tightly fitted in the right places, making movements impossible, making it impossible to think of anything other than the impossibility of action, the impossibility of seeing beyond the smokescreen raised by counter-initiatory ideologies, far from gnosis, far from any logic.

To the more discerning eye, it inevitably resembles a factory.

It's like a reverse assembly line: instead of creating something useful from little, it takes what is already perfect, what is divine, and distorts it in the worst possible ways.

What was once harmonious, sensible, round, complete, is reflected in a distorting funhouse mirror, completely altering the image.

Immersing yourself in this reflection fractures you at your very essence, as if you were diving among glass molecules, shattering your soul and reducing you to a horrific frozen fractal formed by demonic vibrations.

It's, precisely, a production. Notably, before every show produced by, for example, Netflix, the trademark "A NETFLIX ORIGINAL, "A Netflix Production" appears, almost trying to confer a sort of legitimacy to what you're about to see, or justification. It's like trying to look good, like a peacock displaying its colorful wheel.

And here lies the substantial difference: an Artist CREATES, a company PRODUCES.

In these shows, you never recognize the director, nor the cinematographer, nor an idea that isn't imbued with some corrupted ideal, you don't recognize the hand of who should be an artist because the "artists" have abandoned this role to become tradesmen.

It's all excessively ornate, usually featuring some pretty face incapable of acting, perhaps some actor in vogue at that given moment, with relentless advertising in every frame, to mask the evident lack of form and substance.

After all, you would never swallow a poison pill if it weren't coated in honey hiding its true horrendous odor and lethal taste.

The honey, in this circumstance, crystallizes in the forms of "music," "cinema", TV series... Every ideology is veiled, sweetened, made accessible, consumable, promoted, shareable by the multitude, assimilated, but never truly metabolized.

You can't metabolize poison, and just like a symbiont that appropriates your resources, you yourself become the monstrous creature.

A parasite never kills the body that hosts it, otherwise, it would die in turn.

So it drains every last drop of your energy, leaving you with only the bare minimum to survive and continue propagating crude ideas, ecstatic at the discovery of a subculture, you become both its champion and subject simultaneously.

Unwittingly immersed in this context, people base their tastes and habits on what is offered to them by various streaming platforms or television (offered based on algorithms and/or current trends, let it be clear).

A trend doesn't stand the test of time, genius does. For the same reason, Shakespeare is still read, while the latest Marvel films will only be remembered for their box office earnings.

In fact, I challenge anyone who uses these platforms to name the last productions they watched. Not only will they not remember even half of them, as they lack any artistic relevance, form, and thought, but insidiously they will have contributed to the general corruption of the subject (and object) in question.

It's no coincidence that the favorite "singers" of the masses are those who most often participate in festivals, such as the Sanremo Festival in Italy.

A festival that should be "about music", by definition, but is nothing more than a huge think tank, containing all the ideologies and trends that will be perpetuated and reiterated in the coming year.

Something famous only because it's famous. Something unacceptable, especially for music lovers.

Because, you must accept it, music is found elsewhere.

Anyone who participates in such festivals is often a product of the industry, a character constructed through some "talent" and exploited until it is decided that the fashion must change, pushing new faces and relegating the old ones (only 2-3 years old, mind you) to oblivion.

In this regard, "talent shows" should not even exist.

Genius is universally recognized over time. What the "talent show" does is amputate an artist's improvement process and feed them to the masses as they are, setting a new standard for anyone who is a creator or consumer of the art in question.

If a singer is awarded in the most famous talent show in the country where it takes place, that particular artist will be the pivot around which all future music production will revolve until a new "winner" is elected, launching a new trend and so on.

But who could legitimize the criteria by which a certain artist is awarded in a certain talent show?

Who awarded them?

Who can prove that there was no manipulation by the program's producers?

Would the same winner have won in another talent show?

An even more legitimate and relevant question, on what authority should a talent show dictate the direction that art should follow from that moment on and decide to reward only those who conform to it?

Mussolini said: "Art belongs to the domain of the individual."

And he was a dictator.

In this (re)cycle, who do you think represents the music of your country is nothing but a spokesperson.

Introducing passive consumers to the writings of Masaru Emoto ('The Hidden Messages in Water', 2004), which discuss the effects of words and music on us, in other words, what vibrates, could be effective.

As Nikola Tesla suggested, to penetrate the secrets of the universe, one must conceive it in terms of energy, frequency, and vibration.

Everything that exists vibrates. Even if we are not aware of it, even a rock vibrates. Our inability to perceive it would stem from the fact that such vibration falls outside our audible range, between 20 and 20,000 hertz. Beyond this range, humans cannot perceive vibrations.

Returning to Emoto's experiments, in short, he would freeze water and analyze the resulting crystals under a microscope, photographing them.

He found that fractals exposed to low-quality music or negative words appeared broken, incomplete, and distorted.

Conversely, fractals generated by positive energies took on magnificent, complete, primitive shapes, just like the sounds of nature, which always prove to be perfect.

It's no coincidence that some of our words regarding weather or natural events mimic the primal sound of the event itself, and for this reason, they are similar in all languages of the world.

"Not by chance," Emoto says, "the words 'mood' and 'humidity' derive from the same Latin word. Even the ancients realized that, with enough water, people have lighter hearts and can appreciate humor, while this tends to disappear when humidity decreases."

We could therefore deduce that water, charged with positive vibrations, becomes a vehicle and receptacle for happiness and well-being, or the exact opposite.

Now, being composed of 60% water, you can easily understand how vulnerable your integrity is to the kind of vibrations you are exposed to.

Make your choice.

The discourse, as mentioned, extends to various branches of the entertainment industry.

I love cinema, but I have a deep contempt for the Oscars; it is an elitist circle where billionaires congratulate themselves, awarding themselves, not coincidentally, in 99% of cases, American productions like the infamous 'Top Gun' (by the way, funded and promoted by the US Navy and the Department of Defense - it's evident how the act of rewarding such ideologies sends a message to the rest of the world: "if you're not on our side, we are well justified in bringing OUR democracy to your country, with bombs").

It is interesting to note how the latest films self-proclaimed as winners have been 'Oppenheimer' (a film about the atomic bomb) and 'Barbie' (feminist propaganda of the worst kind).

Regarding my last statement, I feel it's necessary to clarify my positions.

Even a child would hope that both parents (mother and father) enjoy the same rights.

I express my dismay towards those who have taken 'Barbie' as a symbol of feminist propaganda.

It's a ridiculous attitude incompatible with any legitimate concept of pure feminism.

The same doll has ingrained in the collective memory the stereotype of the "perfect" woman: tall, blonde, with blue eyes.

Any further variation of the aforementioned is not aimed at inclusivity and representation but rather at increasing sales of gadgets even among those who don't fit that model.

One could deduce, therefore, that any further variation in contemporary taste does not aim at taste per se but at inclusivity and representation of minority groups who would like greater rights than all other living beings.

The minority groups in question would like, in addition to increased and inviolable rights (but only for themselves), the possibility of enjoying every vice that would best represent them.

Have we not legitimized the buying and selling of children? Various institutions offer the questionable practice of "gestation for others" (avoiding the term "surrogate motherhood" to align with current policies), with prices varying depending on the characteristics of newborns, such as hair and eye color (blonde girls with blue eyes are the most expensive! – ironic, considering the aforementioned Barbie case).

And have we not considered the idea and possibility of aborting during the ninth month of pregnancy? At this rate, I expect that soon the bill will be presented to the unborn child before decapitating it with the cry of "Freedom!"

Let it be clear; it's more than legitimate to interrupt a pregnancy if it's the rotten fruit of violence.

But this shouldn't allow anyone to speak of a fetus as a bag that we can get rid of, absolving ourselves of any moral responsibility.

Anyone who speaks lightly of aborting a soul has lost their divine spark, has become someone or something totally integrated, assimilated, and represented but dispersed in the material world. Someone who ignores divine mechanisms, something that exists only because there is space in the world.

"My body is mine, and I decide what to do with it," is the mantra.

However, it seems that this principle only holds until experimental gene therapies are imposed en masse, violating every state of law and the fundamental rights of every human being.

Aside from this massive contradiction, the concept is correct.

But what about the body of "the other"? That body is what you were, what I was, what we all were.

If, through your negligence, you did not take the necessary precautions to avoid pregnancy, with what lack of spirit and understanding of the divine could you think of absolving yourself of all responsibility?

This is nothing but the product of the much-touted (and fake) democracy. A democracy that deludes itself about its own freedom by granting permission to carry out crazy acts, like "changing" biological sex or even denying it, but which, ironically, censors any doubt raised against them.

It's a democracy that denies the freedom to express divergent thoughts, labeling in the most despicable way anyone who dares to deviate from the regime's narrative.

In this regard, a lesson in style is offered by Steven Spielberg with his 'The Post'. A cinematographic gem that highlights the pure figure of Woman.

The film, in its final stages, presents an image of a world that has now ceased to exist:

"The Founding Fathers gave the free press the protection it must have to fulfill its essential role in our democracy. The press serves those who govern, not those who are governed."

CHAPTER III

THE EXTERMINATING ANGEL

What I contest, therefore, is the lack of intellectual honesty in recognizing that there is no longer the will to seek and refine one's taste, to look beyond one's mediocre comforts, beyond the first page of Netflix, and beyond the music charts.

Basing one's taste on rankings and trends is as foolish as those who rely on them. One should not legitimize a thought just because it is widely adopted by the multitude. There would be countless inconvenient examples starting from the Ptolemaic theory, but I would like to avoid dwelling too much on this point.

As previously mentioned, it is more than legitimate and vital for spiritual refinement to make comparisons between various works of ingenuity.

However, I believe that this approach can be extended to all spheres of life: if you only know the light of the sun, you will ignore the moonlight, assuming that the sun is always the only source of illumination.

Likewise, if you only have access to one version of the facts on an issue, you might take it for granted and accept it as absolute truth without considering other perspectives.

I wish to offer examples not only to support my arguments but also to continue in my mission to share what I consider to be inherently beautiful. When it comes to promoting Art, in every form I know, I always do so with great pleasure.

A cinematographic work that has gone unnoticed, unknown to the general public but beloved by cinema lovers, is 'The Exterminating Angel' (El ángel exterminador), directed by Luis Buñuel in 1962.

When I recommend this work to a contemporary, I notice a reluctant grimace of distrust because the film is in black and white. The excuse for not enjoying the beauty of such works lies in phrases like "but it's old," "I don't like black and white films," "old films bore me."

Here lies a big fallacy, which I believe could hinder anyone's interest in art if they decide to become its advocate.

I don't understand how one can consider a film old just because it's in black and white. Limiting the color palette to its extremes could be a stylistic choice (otherwise, we wouldn't have recent works in black and white), or it could be motivated by the symbolism present in the film.

We know how black and white have been used not only in painting but also in the mere descriptive and atavistic field of religious iconography, and beyond.

A superstitious fable described the difference between the two colors in iconographic vision as follows: a bird, the crow, to be precise, was as white as the robe of Christ but decided to start telling lies. God, therefore, reproached him for his excessive arrogance exclaiming, "From now on, you will be as black as the night, just as black as your soul is," and threw a charred piece of wood at him, leaving a large dark stain on his plumage that was impossible to remove.

From that day on, crows were black.

The other logical flaw lies in their consideration of aging.

Something from 50 years ago is considered old because people have become accustomed (not me, mind you) to regurgitating superfluous information every hour, new trends every week, and new faces to inspire them (I renew my exemption from this disastrous mechanism) every couple of years.

It is surprising, however, to note that most people line up to see the 'Mona Lisa', despite it being much older than the mentioned film.

But why does this happen? Mainly for the reasons I have already explained, especially the influence of tastes shaped by rankings.

It is important to clarify that Leonardo's work is objectively of excellent quality and superior to the vast majority of all other existing artistic creations.

However, how many people actually know why the Mona Lisa has become so famous? As mentioned, we cannot ignore the undisputed quality of Leonardo's work, but I could easily cite another of his works of superior quality, present in the same museum where the Mona Lisa is housed (the Louvre in Paris): the 'Virgin of the Rocks' (1483-1486. A second version of the painting is currently present at the National Gallery in London).

It is extraordinary to note how this work seems almost overlooked compared to the famous 'Mona Lisa'. To better understand the situation, a little excursion is necessary.

During the early 1500s, precisely in 1503, Francesco del Giocondo, a Florentine silk merchant, commissioned Leonardo da Vinci to paint a portrait of his wife, Lisa Gherardini, also known as Lisa del Giocondo, from which the name "Mona Lisa" later derived.

However, we know that the work was never delivered to the commissioners, and there is a big shadow of perplexity over the reasons.

The first thesis, widely accepted, suggests that Leonardo was a perfectionist and did not complete the painting before 1517, well over ten years after the start of the creation, leading "the Giocondo" to withdraw from the commission.

The second thesis argues that the commissioners could no longer afford to pay for the painting, so Leonardo kept it. I find this rather unlikely.

The Giocondo family belonged to high society, so I strongly doubt they could no longer afford the finances to pay for a painting they themselves commissioned (I would like to remind you that being immortalized by an artist was in itself a clear representation of high status in society).

A third thesis suggests that Leonardo himself realized the extraordinary value of the work and refused to deliver it. There are studies that demonstrate why the Mona Lisa's smile is so enigmatic: simply put, it's not a smile. But it's something about to become one. It was an early approach to conceptual art, I dare say.

At his death, Leonardo was in France, and his favorite pupil, Salai, inherited his art collection. Consequently, Salai sold the work to the reigning King, Francis I.

But why is the Mona Lisa now so famous? Well, because it was stolen.

An Italian, Vincenzo Peruggia, during the morning of August 21, 1911, snuck into the Louvre (where the work had resided since 1798 when it was transferred from the Palace of Fontainebleau) and stole the painting.

It was only recovered in 1913.

The theft immediately turned the case into a huge media scandal, involving international press coverage during the process. From that moment on, the fame of the Mona Lisa grew exponentially.

My previously stated theses are confirmed, especially when we consider some details.

The first is that, yes, Leonardo's work is extraordinary, but there are copyists who have created identical versions of it.

The second detail, which supports my previous statement, is the presence of another 'Mona Lisa', exhibited at the Prado Museum in Madrid, hence the name 'La Gioconda del Prado', which exhibits a quality comparable to that attributed to Leonardo.

It is hypothesized that this work may have been created by one of his students, after 1519, after Leonardo's death. The 'Gioconda del Prado' appears much more "alive" if we consider the chromatic scale, but not because it is more recent (as mentioned, it was created shortly after the original), but because it has undergone restoration or conservation interventions, things that Leonardo's 'Mona Lisa' cannot enjoy due to its iconicity and recognizability in the collective imagination.

The various cracks, the slightly yellowish and less vivid tone of the canvas, and other details of this kind are now intrinsic characteristics of Leonardo's work.

Furthermore, not only will Leonardo's Mona Lisa not be restored for ethical reasons, but also for economic reasons. The industry of Mona Lisa-themed gadgets, such as t-shirts, mugs, and posters, is extremely vast, and a restoration would entail a total change in the colors and characteristics of the work, influencing its commercial value and the iconic image that the 'Mona Lisa' represents for the masses.

It is important to understand that artists often worked in workshops at the time, where talented young apprentices contributed to their masters' commissions.

It is not excluded that significant parts of the 'Mona Lisa', such as the backgrounds, were painted by Leonardo's apprentices rather than the artist himself.

Those less acquainted with the matter are scandalized by this reality, but it was a very common practice at the time. Some masters even had their apprentices entirely create the works, then signed them in their own names, taking credit for them.

To be honest, I myself consider this practice to be at odds with my perception of Art. For me, this modus operandi resembles a factory or a multinational corporation like Netflix. The workforce is made up of craftsmen, and upon completion, the work is signed by the one who commissioned it.

The result may be artistic, but who is the artist? This question would require another essay to dissect its essence.

Who knows!

CHAPTER IV

ΚΑΛΌΣ ΚΑΊ ἈΓΑΘΌΣ

Now, it cannot be denied that there is no universal beauty. Plato already suggested this in the Symposium, giving voice to the participants of the "banquet" to distinguish between common beauty and divine beauty. He himself argued that everything that resides on Earth is nothing more than a blurred reflection of true universal beauty, of which we only enjoy a tiny fraction.

Since I have been honest so far, I cannot refrain from continuing to be so.

It must be recognized that circumscribing the concept of "beauty" is an objectively difficult task, as the origin of the word itself eludes our understanding.

We must therefore rely on lines of thought that I personally consider the most reliable, applicable, and shareable.

In fact, we (the Italian people, and beyond) are more Greek than we think. Unconsciously, we have assimilated the philosophy of "kalòs kai agathos", meaning we consider beautiful what is good. "Good" not only in moral terms but also in plastic terms.

A universal example can be the expression "what a beautiful road!". Clearly, we are not referring to it as a Bouguereau painting (I would consider that an audacious statement), but as something that embodies the promise for which the road was built.

Our grandparents might have called "beautiful" a road that improved the connection with the city center, facilitated the daily receipt of the newspaper, or the delivery of milk and eggs, but which we now consider decaying and dilapidated because it no longer carries those qualities within it.

The examples could be endless: "what a beautiful hammer," "what a beautiful plate of pasta", and so on.

But here, couldn't my detractors object that I am admitting the existence of subjectivity? This is true, yes, but we are not talking about works of art. As mentioned in the first chapter, you can like everything.

There are coprophages who would gladly exchange a hazelnut cream for their favorite dish, and there are no criteria to give reason to those who might contest their preference. But we, as mentioned, are talking about art, language, rules. Not for nothing in any art manual that respects itself, its "fundamentals" will be mentioned.

CHAPTER V

ANTI-INTELLIGENCE

Recognizing my almost total resignation in the face of mediocrity, I have relegated supporters of so-called "artificial intelligence" as a tool for creating art to an even lower level.

In the fields where I operate, namely contemporary art, the whole issue is becoming the new God. And we know well what happens when the possibility of doubting something is excluded, as has happened in recent times: science, when not subject to review, becomes dogma.

Let it be clear, I am not a passéist as it might seem. I am grateful to the West for some of its discoveries and inventions, which have certainly facilitated the lives of painters and others. A car, for me, is a fantastic observatory. But not more than that (among other things, at some point, even oil painting will be seen as a new medium. Should they have banned it arbitrarily? Clearly not).

However, I must contest the constant development of the issue in directions that are questionable, to say the least. A distinction is needed between the term "progress" and the term "development".

A romantic relationship can DEVELOP into a breakup. On the contrary, by definition, it could PROGRESS into a marriage or into an even closer collaboration between those involved.

For me, a West that invents an atomic bomb capable of pulverizing the entire civilization is not progressing. On the contrary, progress aims at humanity, not at its destruction.

That's why I consider, as mentioned earlier, the possibility of changing one's gender to be a vice that goes beyond all logic. Being able to do so is not progress; it is a development of humanity in the wrong direction, towards its annihilation - not only in plastic terms but also in consciousness terms.

If you cannot identify and recognize your body in matter, something trivial and simple, it means you have got everything wrong. And you go even more wrong when you decide to try to play God.

I could detonate every argument in favor of artificial intelligence as a tool for creating art, saying that there cannot be intelligence where there is no consciousness. A hammer cannot be intelligent, but the invention of it or the use that one decides to make of it can be intelligent.

The average detractor will say, "So a tree is not intelligent," and you can only laugh and walk away. Demand that this subject not exist, because it is probably true. Not recognizing the intelligent design behind every living form is a symptom of total blindness to evidence. It is a symbol of complete lack of reasoning, so avoid wasting time.

Perhaps these detractors are unaware that modern science has not yet been able to prove that consciousness is directly inherent in the brain. Consciousness resides elsewhere and is confined to living beings. So a machine with a mechanical brain will not be conscious and therefore cannot be, by definition, intelligent.

And still, perhaps people are forgetting (or have never known) the origin of the term "robot". "Robot" comes from a Czech term "robota", which means "hard work".

I fail to comprehend how we managed to completely ignore the meaning of the term to our disadvantage and apply the presence of these machines as our prostheses for any kind of activity. Heart rate monitors, virtual reality headsets (as if there isn't already a reality in which you are immersed from the moment you are conceived), sleep measurement tools (as if listening to your body isn't enough to know if you are tired or not), and so on.

A modern example of this complete decay and corruption of the spirit is accepting "Alexa", the perfect embodiment of Orwell's 'Big Brother' who sees and hears everything.

"But no, it doesn't hear you. It only responds if you call it."

And would you believe me if I told you that a dead person answered my questions directed to them? A dead person has only one way to answer questions: not being dead.

To be honest, 'Alexa' behaves like 90% of people, therefore unconsciously. In fact, I believe that by installing the chip containing "Alexa's" knowledge into a human host body, it could perform even better than the human itself. Or at least, in the same way. Worrisome. For the human in question.

As mentioned, this is for me an opportunity to not only bring you closer to the truth but also an excellent opportunity to recommend works for you to watch.

I would like to reaffirm my beliefs by talking about an excellent documentary from 2012, "The Never-Ending Man", directed by Kaku Arakawa (I would emphasize the word MAN used - not "machine").

Miyazaki decides to create a short animated film, before definitively abandoning his career (a decision that will not happen at that time, but rather, he will make a beautiful film called 'The Boy and the Heron', 2023, years later).

After drawing and defining the subject and plot, he decides to entrust the animation of the short film to Studio Ghibli.

However, here he is presented with a rather controversial idea. Some members of Studio Ghibli show him how artificial intelligence could "animate" his creation, eliciting a reaction of outrage from him. Needless to describe how he expressed his displeasure, but he arrived at a conclusion that I myself would like to reiterate:

"The Human Race has lost confidence in itself".

CHAPTER VI

DIVINE SPARK

I conclude this brief essay with a message of hope, for both the creative and the non-creative.

You will NEVER be replaced by machines.

Artificial intelligence, an oxymoron in itself, cannot invent anything new.

In the creative realm, what it does (or rather, what we allow it to do) is consider your inputs, take all the data it "knows," mix them, and produce an output.

In the non-creative realm, the story is the same. For the same reason, a machine cannot, as mentioned, invent anything. It cannot develop a formula for interplanetary travel, discover a cure for a disease, or create an artistic composition without drawing from pre-existing images, which, needless to say, are the product of human ingenuity.

For this reason, we will never see it founding an artistic movement, such as fauvism, neoclassicism, suprematism, dadaism, and so on.

Therefore, while the machine possesses exceptional computing power, decidedly superior to ours, it lacks inventiveness. This is because every calculation is based on available data, such as calculating the square root of a very large number or counting the accidents that occurred in New York in the last few months.

The examples are endless.

However, upon careful consideration, these deductions lead me to an inevitable, tragicomic conclusion.

Artificial intelligence does not exist.

Given that intelligence does not reside in machinery, where would the difference lie between a contemporary machine and one from a few years or decades ago?

There is no difference. Let us put an end to this dull debate now.

As I said before, progress is directed towards humanity, not its obliteration.

However, a robot lacks humanity, so it cannot progress.

If a contemporary juicer is more efficient than one from a few decades ago, it is not because of the juicer itself, but because of the adjustments made by humans to improve the object in question.

Humans devise a system to better operate the blades, apply it (input), and the machine executes it (output). What would have been intelligent about the machine?

Again,

THERE IS NO INTELLIGENCE WHERE THERE IS NO CONSCIOUSNESS.

We have therefore outlined the strong points of the machine in question, such as the computing power that allows it to show us the way on the navigator. But this is nothing that humans couldn't do as well. Perhaps you've forgotten the maps that were used before the advent of the "tom-tom"?

Therefore, we can delineate the limitations of a machine, but how can you circumscribe human ingenuity?

Creativity cannot be measured, calculated, or extracted from nothing. It is innate, a personal construction formed from streams of consciousness and knowledge invisible even to the most advanced machine. And I am not afraid of being replaced by a machine.

I am a Human, a human being. I possess the divine spark that a machine can never enjoy.

CHAPTER VI

NEBULOUS VIBRATIONS

The best method to represent a state of mind is to let it flow freely into forms without constraints. In our minds, these feelings appear as star formations, bursts of color, and nebulous vibrations.

We would define the whole as an abstract constellation.

The feeling is defined, but its "plastic" representation rarely will be-unless one wishes to risk falling into a banal figurativism of the human body.

This is precisely why I believe abstraction is the most faithful representation of what is true, what is real.

An example proves my thesis true is the following: Imagine yourself in front of a set of brushes and objects, ready to leave a mark on a flat, two-dimensional surface, along with a tin bucket containing ink.

If I asked you to leave a mark with these materials, it would be the exact representation of your current condition.

If you were sad or angry, the marks would be less rich in ink but full of straight lines and well-defined marks, perhaps dotted and concentrated in a limited area.

On the other hand, if you were happy, the marks would be softer, rounder, comma-shaped, finding themselves, and the ink would be used sparingly across the entire available surface.

It is not possible to define a sensation, so we must allow it to define itself.

Colors carry with them primordial, innate feelings. Movement is closely linked to the emotion in question.

The centrifugal and centripetal forces present in them are accentuated by color and inevitably coexist and resonate within us.

Abstract art is abstract only in its representation, not in its intention. Not in its nature.